KING ST.

Set Three
BOOK 4

The Party

The Party
King Street: Readers Set Three - Book 4
Copyright © Iris Nunn 2014

Text: Iris Nunn
Editor: June Lewis

Published in 2014 by Gatehouse Media Limited

ISBN: 978-1-84231-129-5

British Library Cataloguing-in-Publication Data:
A catalogue record for this book is available from the British Library

It was wet all day Saturday.
Jill had had a hard day
at the shop.
She had nothing in for tea.

"Get some fish and chips, Jill,"
Dave said to her.

Jill did not want to go out,
but she did not want to cook.
So she went to the fish and chip shop.

When she got there
she had to wait.
She had to wait for the fish.

In front of her was a woman.
"I have seen that face before,"
Jill said to herself.

"I hate this rain,"
said the woman.

"Me too," said Jill.

"I think you live at number six,"
said the woman.

"That's right," said Jill.

"We have just moved
into number three,"
said the woman.

"Number three,
over the road from me?"
asked Jill.

"That's right," said the woman.
"Hey, would you like
to come to a party?
We are having
a house-warming party."

"When is it?" said Jill.

"Next Saturday at 7.30."

"That will be fine," said Jill.
"Thanks a lot.
By the way, my name is Jill."

"And I am Sharon,"
said the woman.

When Jill got home
she told Dave about the party.

"Do I have to go?" he said.
"I do not like parties."

"Come on Dave.
I do like to get out.
You will have a good time too."

On Saturday Jill and Dave
went over to number three.
They took wine with them,
red wine.

Jill rang the bell.
Sharon came to the door.
"I am glad to see you, Jill.
You are the first."

"This is Dave.
Dave, meet Sharon," said Jill.

Inside the house, Sharon said,
"Meet my husband, Mick."

The bell rang.
Sharon went to the door.

"Here's some wine," said Dave
and handed Mick a bottle.

"Thanks, Dave," said Mick.
"Would you like a drink?"

Dave asked for beer.
Jill asked for wine.
"A glass of red wine, please."

Mick went to get the drinks.

Jill saw some photos on a shelf.
She looked at the photos.
She looked at one photo,
an old photo.
It was an old school photo.

"Dave, look at this photo.
This is my old school
and this is me!"

Sharon came over.
She looked at the photo, too.

"This is you?
Well, this is me.
We must have been at school
together.
You must be Jill Lewis.
I am Sharon Dawson."

"Well I never!" they both said.